PRESENTED TO:

_____

FROM:

_____

Let My Prayer Be Set Forth Before You As Incense

(Psalm 141:2 NKJV)

Melissa Noel Wassum

WestBow Press books may be ordered through booksellers or by contacting:

WestBow Press
A Division of Thomas Nelson & Zondervan
1663 Liberty Drive
Bloomington, IN 47403
www.westbowpress.com
844-714-3454

Because of the dynamic nature of the Internet, any web addresses or links contained in this book may have changed since publication and may no longer be valid. The views expressed in this work are solely those of the author and do not necessarily reflect the views of the publisher, and the publisher hereby disclaims any responsibility for them.

Interior Image Credit: Melissa Noel Wassum

Scripture marked (NKJV) taken from the New King James Version®. Copyright © 1982 by Thomas Nelson. Used by permission. All rights reserved.

Scripture marked (NIV) taken from the Holy Bible, NEW INTERNATIONAL VERSION®, NIV® Copyright © 1973, 1978, 1984, 2011 by Biblica, Inc.® Used by permission. All rights reserved worldwide. -Scripture marked (KJV) taken from the King James Version of the Bible.

Scripture quotations marked (ESV) are from The ESV® Bible (The Holy Bible, English Standard Version®), copyright © 2001 by Crossway, a publishing ministry of Good News Publishers. Used by permission. All rights reserved.

ISBN: 978-1-6642-7635-2 (sc)
ISBN: 978-1-6642-7637-6 (hc)
ISBN: 978-1-6642-7636-9 (e)

Library of Congress Control Number: 2022915824

Print information available on the last page.

WestBow Press rev. date: 09/20/2022

Let My Prayer Be Set Forth Before You As Incense

(Psalm 141:2 NKJV)

By Melissa Noel Wassum

Dedicated to…

God, my heavenly Father, who loves me with an everlasting love.

To my mother, who shows me what a Christian life is
and who led me to Christ.

And in remembrance of Pastor Robert B. Greene,
Whose prayers inspired my own prayer life.

Simply Pray

Heavenly Father,

Help us to remember that prayer can be as simple as a child's bedtime prayer, a cry for "Help", a moment of gratefulness - "Thank You Jesus", or even a shed tear in silence.

We know You just long to hear from us as any parent longs to hear from their children. And any time spent with You is quality time. You always give Your best to us. May we honor You with our time by keeping in touch always.

It's so amazing to think that the prayers of all of God's people are like incense and are collected in golden bowls in heaven.

Thank You for listening to us.

Thank You for our Lord Jesus, Who taught us how to pray.

May we pray without ceasing.

Amen

Prayer to the Father

Heavenly Father,

We honor You as the Living God and Creator of all things.

May we always acknowledge You and know that You will direct our paths.

Thank You Father for blessing us, for we know that every good gift is from above.

May we give generously, for we know that the measure we use will be measured back to us.

Thank You Father for forgiving us of our sins.

May we be kind and compassionate to one another, forgiving offenses made against us.

Father, we don't fully understand all that is going on in the world, but we will not fear for You are in control.

May we live, boldly confessing Christ who's Holy Spirit lives in us.

Be near us, Lord Jesus our Savior.

Amen

Prayer for A Good Father

We love you so very much, Father God.

Thank you for sending your Son Jesus to show us how You love us.

Thank you for His sacrifice that redeems us to You.

We are so sorry when we fail You with our sinful nature.

But we are so grateful for the precious blood of Christ which covers our sins, and the promise of our salvation.

We thank You for all Your many blessings and ask for solutions to our problems.

You are a good Father who always provides for His children.

Thank you for your Holy Spirit that dwells in us; may we always be a welcome home.

Thank you for your Holy Word, and may it reveal to us all about You and nourish us daily.

We pray for courage to seek the lost and to tell them about Your great love.

We lift up each person who has crossed our path this week to You.

Help us to be spiritual doctors who work to bring Your healing to the spiritually sick/lost people in our community, and to find ways to invite them to Your table.

Amen

A Prayer for When

My Father God in Heaven,

When I am hungry, You feed me through Your Word.

When I am thirsty, You fill me with springs of Living Water.

When I am tired, You give me rest.

When I am weak, You are strong.

When I am anxious, You tell me not to worry – You've got this.

When I am afraid, You tell me to fear not.

When I feel all alone, You remind me You are with me always.

When I don't know where to go, You show me You are the Way.

When I can't go on any further, You carry me.

When I feel like I can't do it anymore, You say "Lay your burdens at my feet."

When I don't know…

    When or

    Where or

    What or

    How or

    Why,

You, Father, are the answer.

Amen.

You're in Control

Lord God,

Sometimes we can scarcely handle all that life throws our way. But we're grateful that you understand our thoughts, and that You are with us regardless of how we feel.

Help us to trust You and to keep trusting You in spite of how things appear. For You oh God are our ever present help in times of trouble.

Father, give us peace in this place. Help us to lean on You. Strengthen us with Your strong right hand. And remind us You are in Control.

There is no cause for shame, because we know Whom we have believed and are convinced that He is able to guard what we entrusted to Him until that day.

Father, we glorify Your holy name and thank You for Your many blessings.
And as we have forgiven others, may You forgive us for our sins.
We pray for those in need, that You would provide.
We pray for those who are ill, that You would heal them.
We pray for Your Kingdom to be established on Earth as it is in heaven.
Glory to God in the highest.
Amen

Someday…

Heavenly Father,

I imagine that someday we will all stand before Your throne as our Judge. And each person will be accused by the prosecutor, who will give an account of the charges of sin. He will present his case making many vile accusations – crimes of greed, lust, murder, lies, and many other numerous offenses.

And for those who failed to accept Jesus Christ as their Savior before their death, will find they are without council and will try to defend themselves. But they will be found guilty as charged and sentenced to eternal life in torment.

However, for those who have asked Jesus to come into their heart and be their Savior, they will have an Advocate. And when a saint's case is presented, their Defender will object, stating that all charges are false. And He will motion for the case to be thrown out of court.

The Judge will look at the Defender with great love and ask on what grounds the case can be dismissed.

The Defender will submit the Lamb's Book of Life as evidence. Jesus has redeemed the saint and paid the price at the cross for their sin. Every charge made against him/her is false because he/she placed their faith in Jesus.

The bailiff to bring forth the Lamb's Book of Life to the bench. He will present it to the Judge, open to the page where the saint's name is written and sealed with the precious blood of Christ. Upon seeing the name, the Judge questions how the defendant will plead. The Defender offers the plea of not guilty.

The Judge presents the verdict. Because the prosecutor did not prove the defendant is guilty beyond a shadow of a doubt, as all of these sins have been forgiven by Jesus, the saint is not guilty. Case is dismissed.

And our Advocate Jesus will take our hand and guide us up to the Father, who waits with open arms to embrace us. The guilt, shame and separation will be no more. The loving Father welcomes his child home.

No Law and Order episode can compare to this case for your Law cannot be changed and your covenant is true and just. Praise God for Your tender mercy.

We thank You Father for the hope of eternal life with You.

Amen.

Prayer for Abba

Heavenly Father,

We praise Your holy name and give you all the glory and honor for all the great things you have done.

It's difficult to fathom Your great love, but somehow our hearts know through the Holy Spirit and Your Word.

Help us to share this love with others that they will praise You.

We are disheartened by the way things are in our world – divisiveness, sickness, death, broken relationships, greed, lust, murder, self-centeredness; often things we find in ourselves as we struggle with the flesh.

But we know that He who lives in us is greater than he who lives in the world, and we are more than conquerors in Christ Jesus. Praise God.

Father, You tell us to ask and we will receive, so we ask for You to meet our needs – both physical and spiritual.

We hand over our worries to You, knowing You will take care of them so we need not fear.

Bless us abundantly.

Protect us from those who would harm us and from the evil one.

Guide us through your Holy Word.

Forgive us for our sins.

Don't give up on our loved ones who are lost or astray; we give them to You.

Help us to be mighty warriors of faith.

We thank You for Your hope, peace and love.

Thank you for Jesus, the Holy Spirit, and your Holy Word.

Thank you for creation; it is so diverse and amazing.

Thanks Abba.

In Christ's name we pray,

Amen

Prayer for a Gathering

Heavenly Father,

We praise and love You for You are the Living God, Maker of all creation. Redeemer of our souls.

Father, may we never cause someone to stumble, and forgive those who seek forgiveness from us.

May our faith, no matter how great or small, be pleasing to You; for You can do exponentially great things.

May we always obey Your Word, that we would be blessed in all things.

May we always give thanks to You, Father.

May we be prepared for the day of the Lord and remember Jesus' sacrifice for our sins.

May we spread the Good News to others that they may glorify our Father in heaven.

May we yield ourselves so that when others look at us, they see Jesus.

Father, bless and keep us until we meet again.

For it is in Jesus' precious name we pray,

Amen

Resurrection Remembrance Prayer

Heavenly Father,

Our God Who so loved the world that You gave Your one and only Son. That whosoever believes in Him shall not perish but have eternal life. *(John 3:16 NIV)*

And we, your children do believe!

Thank You, Father, for the most extraordinary plan of salvation. That You would be so merciful to us and forgive us for our sins to accept us into Your family through Christ.

We praise You Father, we love You, and we honor You.

Thank you, Jesus, for Your sacrifice and separation from the Father to bear all of our sin and iniquities on the cross. Thank You for being born of a virgin to live among us as the Son of Man, and yet still be God. To feel our weaknesses yet live without sin.

Thank you, Holy Spirit for choosing us as your dwelling place. We are but made of dust and yet so lovingly designed to be completely unique, and utterly known down to our very DNA. Wow! Thank You for Your guidance to draw us nearer to God. Grant us your peace.

We long for the day when we'll be united face to face, but until then forgive us for our sin, bless us this day, and help us to be ambassadors for the Kingdom of God.

We pray this in the name of the Father, the Son, and the Holy Spirit.

Amen

Father, May I..

Heavenly Father,

    May I RUN to You

        When I am afraid.

    May I WALK with You

        Wherever I go.

    May I STAND up for You

        When others reject You.

    May I SIT at Your feet

        And listen to what You say.

    May I LAY down in peace

        While You give me rest.

    And in everything I do,

        May it always BE with You.

    Amen

Father, please carry us

Our Father in heaven,

The great I Am, Who was, and is, and is to come.

We honor and praise You, knowing You are the Living God.

We seek Your guidance for our lives, and ask that You bless us for everything we need.

And when we have burdens that overwhelm us, making us feel like we are sinking in the sea, lost in the desert, consumed by the darkness, or feeling all alone.

We know

You will carry us like a groom carries his bride over the threshold,

You will carry us like an expectant mother carries her child close to her heart in her womb,

You will carry us like a father carries his tired child on his shoulders.

For even to our old age, You are He Who will sustain us. You have made us. You will carry us. You will rescue us.

We need not fear anything life throws at us, because You are for us and not against us.

We praise You Father God for this blessed assurance.

Thank you.

Amen

Father, We….

Heavenly Father,

We bless Your holy name.

We pray for Your will to be done.

We ask for You to bless us in our daily needs.

We ask for Your forgiveness.

We pray for Your strength against temptation.

We praise and honor You with all glory.

Bless our nations, our church, our family, and friends.

Amen

Seasons Change

Heavenly Father,

It's so amazing how there is sustaining order in your creation. I consider how the seasons change, to how our lives are fulfilled.

SPRING – is like when we are born and life begins

SUMMER – is like how we grow and live

FALL – is like how we fall into sin

WINTER – is like when we die spiritually. But if we accept Christ as our Savior, he covers our sin like snow

SPRING – that we may be reborn again and SPRING to everlasting life.

I pray that all would be saved in Christ Jesus.

Amen

Prayer From Your Children

Heavenly Father,

How can we ever think to approach You but for your glorious grace, that You would forgive our sins by the blood of Jesus and see His sacrifice as holy and pleasing to You.

And through acceptance of Him as our Savior, You adopt us as Your children so we can call you Father. Praise God!

Father, we thank You for being so very gracious to us.

Thank You for our family and friends, our homes, food, clothing, transportation.

Thank you for our pets, for the colors of Spring – as what was dormant is springing back to life; a very easy way to have faith in the Resurrection.

We pray for those who don't know and for those who refuse to believe.

Father, there is so much going on in our personal lives, at our work, in the world, that causes us pain, struggle or fear. We lay these at Your feet for we know You are in control, and You are for us Father.

Faith but the size of a mustard see can move mountains.

Father, bless us that we may be a blessing to others; may we never be a hindrance to Your kingdom.

Father, we honor You, we thank You, we love You.

In Jesus' name we pray,

Amen

And All God's People Say... Amen

Father God in heaven,

We love you with all our hearts, with all our souls, and with all our might.

For you Lord God are holy. May we glorify your name forever.

May we seek first the Kingdom of God and Your righteousness.

Father, we know that You are able to bless us abundantly, so that in all things, at all times, having all that we need, You, will abound in every good work. Thank you for being so generous to us.

But like the Apostle Paul, we too "have the desire to do what is right, but not the ability to carry it out." (*Romans 7:18 English Standard Version*). However, You, have given us a spirit not of fear, but of power, and love, and self-control. May we yield ourselves to His direction.

May we forgive others as you have forgiven us. For "He himself bore our sins in His body on the tree, that we might die to sin and live to righteousness. By His wounds we have been healed."

Father, we lift up in prayer all of those in need.

May Your word be hidden in our hearts that we may not sin against Thee.

And all God's people say…

Amen

How to Pray

Our Lord, Jesus Christ, gave us a beautiful guide on how to pray to God our Father – The Lords' Prayer.

Salutation

    Our Father which art in heaven

Honor/Reverence

    Hallowed by Thy name

Submission to His Authority

    Thy kingdom come, Thy will be done in earth, as it is in heaven

Trust/Requests

    Give us this day our daily bread, And forgive us our trespasses

Obedience

    As we forgive those who trespass against us

Guidance

    And lead us not into temptation

Faith/Protection

    But deliver us from evil

Hope

    For Thine is the kingdom, and the power, and the glory, forever and ever.

Agreement

    Amen

(Matthew 6:9-13 KJV)

Prayer is how we communicate with God. We are instructed to "pray without ceasing" (1 Thessalonians *5:78 New King James Version)*; which means that we should talk with Him often, about everything and anything. God knows everything there is to know about us; he created us uniquely for this particular time and place. He has a plan for our lives; but He wants us to honor Him and for us to allow Him to lead us in the path we should follow. Ask Him and He will answer.

One of His greatest gifts is free will. God is a gentleman. He does not force us to worship him. But if you will accept his Son Jesus as your Savior, he will forgive you of your sin and adopt you into His family as one of His children. And He will become your heavenly Father.

So make sure you call on Him often to talk, He's always available. You just have to pray.

And may your prayers be set forth to the Father, like incense.

Printed in the United States
by Baker & Taylor Publisher Services